Too Much CJ!

Monet Love-Peterson
Illustrated By: Hadiamir Farhan

Design Copyright@2021 by Danyel Ayers

Illustrated By: Hadiamir Farhan

All rights reserved. No part of this publication may be reproduced, stored in a retrieval system or transmitted in any form or by any means, electronic, mechanical, photocopying, recording, or otherwise, without the prior permission of the publisher.

Printed in the Unted States of America
Lulu Press, Morrisville, NC

First time printing: September 2021

ISBN: 978-1-7362209-8-6

To My Nephew/Son Chris Jr.
You have grown so much in knowledge, wisdom and self-control. You have learned the valuable and priceless lessons about structure, boundaries and choices. Thank you for placing value in the life lessons that were poured into you and maturing into a good man.
I love you to the moon and back.
Love always, Aunt Mo (Momma Mo)

CJ is a cute little Yorkie.
His parents don't agree.
Daddy loves to give him
freedom to choose.
Mommy thinks he is too
young and he will loose.

Loose his freedom to run and play
Learning how to balance, not waste the day.
He loves to eat. He loves to play.
and video game the day away.

No structure or boundaries according to dad.
No rules or guidelines need to be had.
Rules from his mom, there is no need to read.
He's loving his life, no need to take heed.

"Why should I read?"
It's boring and long.
I'd rather watch tv even if it is wrong".
"What's wrong with playing? I'll have time to learn.
School is all year, no need for concern.

I can eat what I want!
My dad is the best.
Candy, cookies and cupcakes be my guest!
Treats are great and fill up my tummy.
Cotton Candy, starburst and soda are all yummy.

Too much! What's that?
I can do what I like.
Stay up all night playing games with delight.
I love my dad's rules because there are none.
Living my best life and having much fun.

Too much! What's that?
I can do what I like.
Oh no, I can't get up for school, this is not right.
I went to bed late. I was playing too long.
Fell asleep in class and got the answers wrong.

Oh well, I'll make it up.
I'll get the work done.
After I run and play and have some more fun.
The pop quiz and projects were due at one time,
Preparation is key, but I'll be just fine.

I'm a little worried, because now my teeth hurt.
Went to the dentist and there is a need for alert.
The candy, cookies and sweet gummy treats
Baked five little holes called cavities, too sweet!

Too much sugar, this pain is real.
Those sweet candies did indeed steal,
Steal the fun and the joy I had,
Making my own choices and loving my dad.

In the dentist chair and feeling all this pain,
Our choices are long lasting, here comes the rain.
My tears are raining down my face.
Was the fun worth it?
I need some Grace.

I learned hard lessons
from MY choosing too
much
Too much candy, video
games and other fun
stuff.
Not liking the rules and
guidelines Mom gave,
These assignments and
work load made me cave

Cave in and not have any self-control,
A valuable lesson, the truth be told.
So, if you are given the chance to choose,
Too much of anything and you will lose.

The fun and the treats will always be there,
But, choose wisely and be prepared.
Learn from CJ, some valuable tools.
Everyone needs to follow some rules.